Profiles in American History

The Life and Times of

PAUL REVERE

Mitchell Lane
PUBLISHERS

P.O. Box 196 · Hockessin, Delaware 19707

Profiles in American History

Titles in the Series

The Life and Times of

Alexander Hamilton

Benjamin Franklin

Betsy Ross

Eli Whitney

George Rogers Clark

Hernando Cortés

John Adams

John Cabot

John Hancock

John Peter Zenger

Nathan Hale

Patrick Henry

Paul Revere

Samuel Adams

Sir Walter Raleigh

Susan B. Anthony

Thomas Jefferson

William Penn

Profiles in American History

PAUL REVERE

Jim Whiting

Printing 1 2 3 4 5 6 7 8 9

Library of Congress Cataloging-in-Publication Data
Whiting, Jim, 1943–
The life and times of Paul Revere/by Jim Whiting.
p. cm. — (Profiles in American history)
Includes bibliographical references and index.
ISBN 1-58415-441-1 (library bound: alk. paper)
1. Revere, Paul, 1735–1818—Juvenile literature. 2. Statesmen—Massachusetts—Biography—Juvenile literature. 3. Massachusetts—Biography—Juvenile literature. 4. Massachusetts—History—Revolution, 1775–1783—Juvenile literature. I. Title. II. Series.
F69.R43W45 2006
973.3'311092—dc22

2005028499

ISBN-10: 1-58415-441-1 ISBN-13: 978-1-58415-441-9

ABOUT THE AUTHOR: Jim Whiting has been a remarkably versatile and accomplished journalist, writer, editor, and photographer for more than 30 years. A voracious reader since early childhood, Mr. Whiting has written and edited about 200 non-fiction children's books. His subjects range from authors to zoologists and include contemporary pop icons and classical musicians, saints and scientists, emperors and explorers. Representative titles include *The Life and Times of Franz Liszt, The Life and Times of Julius Caesar, Charles Schulz,* and *The Life and Times of Benjamin Franklin.*

Other career highlights are a lengthy stint publishing *Northwest Runner,* the first piece of original fiction to appear in *Runners World* magazine, hundreds of descriptions and venue photographs for America Online, e-commerce product writing, sports editor for the *Bainbridge Island Review,* light verse in a number of magazines, and acting as the official photographer for the Antarctica Marathon.

He lives in Washington state with his wife and two teenage sons.

PHOTO CREDITS: Cover, pp. 1, 3: Getty Images; pp. 6, 9: North Wind Picture Archives; pp. 12, 15, 21: Corbis; p. 24: Cortney Skinner; p. 28: Getty Images; p. 32: Library of Congress; p. 36: Getty Images; p. 38: U.S. Army Center of Military History; p. 40: Getty Images

PUBLISHER'S NOTE: This story is based on the author's extensive research, which he believes to be accurate. Documentation of such research is contained on page 46.

The internet sites referenced herein were active as of the publication date. Due to the fleeting nature of some web sites, we cannot guarantee they will all be active when you are reading this book.

PLB

Contents

British warships were a familiar sight in Boston Harbor. Boston was the most rebellious colonial city when the British Parliament began imposing taxes in the mid-1760s. Eventually it was placed under military rule.

CHAPTER 1

A Quarrel Snowballs

In the late afternoon of March 5, 1770, Edward Garrick, a sixteen-year-old wig-maker's apprentice in Boston, Massachusetts, began shouting at a British Army officer who was walking nearby. He accused the officer of not paying his master for a haircut. The officer ignored Garrick and continued on his way.

There had been many similar verbal conflicts between the people of Boston and members of the British Army for nearly a year and a half. Hundreds of British troops had landed in Boston in September 1768. Boston had been the American city that most opposed a series of laws recently passed by the British Parliament. King George III had ordered the soldiers to occupy the city and enforce order. The people of Boston resented the intruders. They called the soldiers "Redcoats" because of the scarlet woolen coats they wore. They also called them "lobster backs." Lobsters, which have bright red shells when cooked, were very common in the waters off Boston. Both nicknames were intended as insults.

The British didn't remain silent. "Cowardly rascals" was one of the less offensive terms they'd yell back at the colonists.

Even young children taunted the soldiers. Sometimes the name-calling escalated into fistfights. But that was all. The soldiers were under strict orders not to fire on the colonists.

Hugh White, a soldier who was on guard duty by himself, heard Garrick. He confronted the teenager. The two exchanged words. White struck Garrick with the butt of his musket. Garrick fell to the ground.

The incident attracted the notice of passersby. Dozens gathered around White and yelled at him. Soon the incident went beyond words. Because it was still cold in Boston, ice and snow covered the ground. Some of the bystanders made snowballs and threw them at White.

The mob rapidly increased in size. Church bells began to peal, signaling an emergency.

White was afraid for his life. People began shouting that they wanted to murder him. A stream of missiles—which now included oyster shells, pieces of coal, and chunks of ice in addition to the snowballs—rained down on him. He screamed for help.

Captain Thomas Preston and a group of seven soldiers forced their way through the crowd to join White. Preston tried to return his little group to their barracks. The crush of the mob was too great. They could barely move. An especially large man slammed a soldier named Hugh Montgomery to the ground. According to some witnesses, the man was carrying a heavy club.

Montgomery, very angry, fired his musket. Hearing the gunshot, the other soldiers did the same thing. Their musket balls struck several men in the crowd. Three were instantly killed. Two more died later. The soldiers reloaded their weapons and prepared to fire again. Preston ordered them to stop.

Thomas Hutchinson, the American-born governor of Massachusetts Bay Colony, appeared on the scene. He ordered the mob to go home. The sheriff put Preston in jail. His eight men were also placed under arrest.

The government waited several months for the uproar to die down. Then the soldiers went on trial. John Adams, a prominent Boston citizen who would later became the nation's second president, defended them.

Preston and six of his men were found innocent. Two were convicted of manslaughter. They were punished by having a red-hot iron brand the letter *M* (for *murderer*) onto their thumbs.

Paul Revere's engraving of the Boston Massacre in 1770 inflamed public opinion against the British. It made the incident seem like a cold-blooded killing of colonists. What it does not show is that the large mob of colonists had also attacked the handful of soldiers.

Justice was done—at least on paper. Many colonists believed the soldiers deserved a harsher sentence.

Before the shooting, hatred against the British had been simmering among Boston residents for nearly five years. Some of Boston's most radical citizens, such as Samuel Adams, decided to take advantage of the shooting incident. He gave it a heavily biased name: "The Boston Massacre."

Adams approached Paul Revere, a friend of his. Revere was one of Boston's best silversmiths. He was also a skilled engraver. Adams asked Revere to produce an image of the event. Neither Adams nor Revere was interested in an accurate reproduction of the tragedy. They wanted to show the soldiers in as bad a light as possible.

Revere's illustration shows several British soldiers in an orderly row. They are firing their muskets at point-blank range into the crowd. An officer stands behind them. His sword is raised as if he has just given the command to fire. In a print of the engraving, the soldiers' bright red uniforms and a huge cloud of billowing smoke from the shots are the focal point of the piece.

By contrast, the people of Boston appear peaceful and nonthreatening. The bodies of the men who have been shot lie in pools of their own blood. Nearby, a small dog observes the scene.

Revere's engraving quickly fanned out through the American colonies. It inspired a great deal of outrage against the brutality of British soldiers. This outrage was one of the reasons that open warfare would eventually develop between the two sides.

Even in modern times, Revere's engraving is one of the most famous pictures from the Revolutionary era in American history. People who see the engraving can easily believe that the British were completely at fault. As historian David Hackett Fischer concludes, "The print helped to create an image of British tyranny and American innocence that still shapes our memory of the event."[1] It would not be the only time Paul Revere's hand would shape the course and memory of American history.

A Brief History of Boston

John Winthrop

The first man to settle in what is now Boston was the Reverend William Blackstone, who arrived in 1629. At that time, Boston was a peninsula a little over two miles long. It was connected to the mainland by a narrow strip of land called Boston Neck. The Indians called the peninsula Shawmut. Some Boston businesses still carry that name.

The following year, a group of Puritan colonists led by John Winthrop arrived in Salem, located north of Shawmut. Salem wasn't an ideal site for a settlement. At Blackstone's suggestion, Winthrop visited Shawmut and decided it would be a better place to live. The city was officially founded on September 17, 1630. Winthrop named it Boston, after the English city where he had grown up.

Blackstone probably wished that he hadn't invited Winthrop. The Puritans had fled religious persecution in England. They proved to be just as intolerant as their former oppressors had been. Blackstone moved on. A number of others followed him.

Blackstone had chosen the initial site well. Boston's excellent harbor soon made it the leading port in the colonies. The city became prosperous. It also became a center of intellectual development.

Boston emerged as one of the centers of the movement that eventually brought independence. It continued to thrive after the war. By the early nineteenth century, the peninsula was too small to contain everyone who wanted to live there. The city government began filling in the shallow bays and marshes surrounding the peninsula. Many baseball fans around the country are familiar with Fenway Park, the home of the Boston Red Sox. The word *fen* is another name for "swamp" or "marsh." People who attend Red Sox games are sitting on what used to be a swamp.

Boston remains a vibrant city. Several colleges and universities are located there. Visitors enjoy following the Freedom Trail, which links historic sites connected with the Revolutionary War. Paul Revere's house is part of the trail.

Bordeaux, France, close to where Apollos Rivoire grew up, is known for its vineyards and wineries. Its seeming peace concealed a deep division along religious lines. In the 1700s, the Rivoire family was in danger of being executed for their beliefs.

The Man of the House

Apollos Rivoire (uh-PAH-lohs rih-VWAHR) staggered down the gangplank of the ship that had carried him across the stormy Atlantic Ocean to Boston, Massachusetts. It was the fall of 1715 or the spring of 1716. Apollos, at age thirteen, was alone and three thousand miles from his homeland.

Apollos had grown up near the city of Bordeaux, France, a famous wine-growing region. Before Apollos was born, the Catholic government of France decided to deal harshly with its Huguenots (HYOO-guh-nots), the leading Protestant group in the country. Many of them fled to other countries. Others didn't get the opportunity to leave. They were killed.

The Rivoire family had long been Huguenots. Apollos's parents enjoyed a high standard of living and didn't want to leave their home, but they must have felt that their son would be safer somewhere else.

Apollos's uncle Simon had left several years earlier and settled on the British island of Guernsey. It was natural for Apollos to go to Guernsey to be with his uncle. Simon, however, thought his nephew should continue on to the New World.

When Apollos arrived, Boston was one of the largest cities in the colonies. His family had arranged for him to be an apprentice

to a silversmith named John Coney. Silversmiths worked with silver and gold, turning the precious metals into useful and decorative objects such as silverware, buttons, buckles, and bowls.

Coney met the boy on the wharf and took him home. Apollos proved to be a fast learner. He not only became a good silversmith but also learned how to speak English. Soon he changed his name so that the mostly English-speaking population of Boston could easily pronounce it. He became Paul Revere.

Coney died in 1722. Somehow Revere managed to raise enough money to buy out the rest of his apprenticeship from Coney's widow. He went into business on his own. By 1730, he was doing well enough to move to a new location.

In 1729, he had married Deborah Hitchborn (also spelled *Hichborn*). In December 1734, the couple welcomed their second child and first son. He was named Paul after his father. Eleven more children followed, though only Paul and six others would survive childhood.

Not much is known about Paul's life when he was a boy. There were two types of schools in Boston. Children of the well-to-do attended Latin schools, which prepared them to go to college and have jobs such as ministers, doctors, and lawyers. Nearly everyone else, including Paul, went to writing schools. They learned how to read and write and do simple arithmetic. That was all the education they would need for their jobs. By all accounts, Paul enjoyed reading—a pastime he valued for the rest of his life.

Not all his time was spent in school. His mother's large family had lived in Massachusetts for many years, so Paul had plenty of cousins to play with. He would later name most of his children after them. As the family's oldest son, he had to do daily chores. These chores helped the Revere household function smoothly.

When he was fifteen, Paul and five other boys created the Bell Ringers Agreement. Under its terms, they would ring the heavy bells at Old North Church for two hours once a week. The agreement, which is still on view at the church, contains what is perhaps Paul's first experience with the process of democracy.

"We will Choose a Moderator Every three months whose Business shall be to give out the Changes and other Business

A modern-day silversmith at work. Paul Revere's tools would have been very similar to the ones this man is using. Silver is relatively easy to work, but silversmiths need to use a steady, precise hand to turn out quality work.

as shall be agreed by a Majority of Voices then Present,"[1] reads one clause. "The Members of this Society shall not Exceed Eight Persons and all Differences To be decided by a Majority of Voices"[2] reads another.

From an early age, Paul probably knew that he would become a silversmith. It is likely that he stopped going to school when he was about thirteen and became an apprentice for his father. He quickly mastered his craft. When his father died in 1754, the younger Paul, now nineteen, became the head of the business and the man of the house. He couldn't legally own the shop because of his age. The official owner was probably his mother, but Paul and his brothers, especially Thomas, did the work.

In 1756, Paul had his first taste of military life. The British and the French had long been struggling for control of the North American continent. That year, what became known as the French and Indian War was officially declared. Paul was appointed lieutenant in the Massachusetts militia. The militia tried to capture Crown Point, a fort in New York. The mission failed, and Paul returned home. He hadn't seen any actual combat.

In 1757, Paul married Sarah Orne. He was just twenty-two and Sarah was twenty. Their first child, Deborah, was born in 1758. Their first son, Paul Jr., came along two years later.

Paul was fortunate. Because the business passed directly to him, he didn't have any start-up costs. He established a reputation as one of the town's best silversmiths. While his account books from the first years are lost, most of the ones from 1761 and succeeding years survive. They reveal that he did extremely well for several years. Many ships came to Boston, bringing men and supplies to help in the war effort. There was a lot of money in the city. Many people wanted to spend it on decorative items. Paul was happy to oblige them.

The British won the war in 1763. As sometimes happens, a period of economic depression followed the long and costly war. Revere's business suffered. He nearly lost his home. Fortunately he was able to settle his debt out of court. To provide more income for his family, he learned how to make copper engravings. These engravings were used for such things as book illustrations, business cards, political cartoons, and tavern menus.

He also became a dentist. His services included cleaning teeth and making false teeth, which he fashioned from walrus ivory or teeth from animals. He advertised that "he has fixed some Hundred of Teeth and he can fix them as well as any Surgeon-Dentist who ever came from London, he fixes them in such a Manner that they are not only an Ornament, but of real use in Speaking and Eating; he cleanses the Teeth and will wait on any Gentleman or Lady at their Lodgings."[3]

While he was getting back on his feet financially, the English Parliament began a course of events that would force Revere and the rest of Massachusetts to make some crucial decisions.

The Expulsion of the Huguenots

Martin Luther

The Protestant Reformation—which called for major changes in Catholic Church doctrine—began in Germany in 1517 under the leadership of Martin Luther. By the 1550s, the Reformation had spread to France. Its followers became known as Huguenots. As happened elsewhere, there was a great deal of conflict between Catholics and Protestants. In 1562, more than 1,000 Huguenots were killed by Catholics in the town of Vassey. A decade later, many Huguenot leaders were gathered in Paris for a wedding. They were put to death in what became known as the St. Bartholomew Day Massacre. The killing continued for several days, claiming thousands of additional victims. At the Vatican, the home of the Catholic pope, there was rejoicing at the news. A special medal was issued to "honor" the occasion.

Somehow the Huguenots managed to flourish in spite of the persecutions. The Edict of Nantes, proclaimed in 1598, brought a halt to the killings. Though they resumed a few decades later, there were few victims compared to the previous carnage.

In 1685, the French King Louis XIV decided to ignore the edict. Serious persecutions began again. Many Huguenots were killed. Many more began fleeing the country. The refugees included a number of France's greatest thinkers and skilled craftsmen. Their departure hurt French society and had a huge negative effect on the country's economy.

Most of the refugees managed to find safety in other European countries. Thousands of others crossed the Atlantic Ocean. They settled in the colonies and in Canada. Some of the Huguenots in Canada, now known as Acadians, had one more displacement in store. The British expelled them in 1755, distributing them among their other New World possessions. Some were shipped south as far as Louisiana. Their name, Acadian, soon changed to Cajun, a word still in common use. *Cajun* is especially associated with Louisiana music and cuisine.

The artist who made this famous image of Paul Revere was John Singleton Copley. Copley was this country's first great portrait painter. Copley Square, one of Boston's primary public spaces, is named for him.

CHAPTER 3

The Gathering Storm

King George III and Parliament decided to tax the colonies. After all, the colonies were benefiting from British protection. In 1765, Parliament passed the Stamp Act, which required legal documents and many paper products to bear a stamp. The fees from the stamps would pay for the French and Indian War.

The colonists were outraged. No one had given them an opportunity to vote on the tax. "No taxation without representation" became a popular phrase. There were riots in many of the colonies. In Boston, a mob burned down Governor Hutchinson's house. Tax collectors were attacked. Some were tarred and feathered—a painful, humiliating punishment.

Revere became involved with the protests. He and other men in Boston formed the Sons of Liberty. A secret organization with passwords, it would organize acts of resistance against the British.

The resistance was successful. Colonists refused to buy the stamps, and the Stamp Act was repealed within months. Parliament tried another angle in 1767, passing the Townshend Acts. These laws put duties, or taxes, on many essential items that the British sent to the colonies, including glass, paper, and tea.

The Massachusetts Assembly composed a Circular Letter urging all the colonies not to pay these taxes. The king and Parliament

ordered the Assembly to rescind, or take back, the letter. Seventeen members voted to comply with the order. Ninety-two refused.

More than a dozen Sons of Liberty commissioned Revere to make a silver punch bowl commemorating the event. It would honor "the glorious NINETY-TWO . . . who, undaunted by the insolent Menaces of Victims in Power, from a strict Regard to Conscience, and the LIBERTIES of their Constituents . . . Voted NOT TO RESCIND."[1] Known as the Liberty Bowl, it is one of Revere's most famous creations. He engraved the names of the ninety-two men and symbols of liberty on the bowl. He also made an illustration of the other seventeen men. It shows the devil pushing them toward the entrance to Hell.

The British appointed commissioners to collect the new taxes. The Sons of Liberty retaliated. "When these hated men appeared in Boston, the Sons of Liberty turned out on moonless nights with blackened faces and white nightcaps pulled low around their heads," recounts historian David Hackett Fischer. "More than a few customs commissioners fled for their lives."[2]

Revere organized many of these nighttime "visits." Often he was personally involved. One Boston merchant noted: "Two commissioners were very much abused yesterday when they came out from the Publick Dinner at Concert Hall . . . Paul Revere and several others were the principal Actors."[3]

The British responded to the protests by sending hundreds of troops to Boston. As the transport ships loaded with soldiers tied up to the docks, British warships stayed anchored nearby. They were ready to shoot anyone who opposed the landing.

Revere engraved a picture of the landing and called it *The Insolent Parade.* When people in the other colonies saw the engraving, they grew angry at the British.

Not all the colonists were upset. Many of them still supported the king and Parliament. They called themselves Loyalists. The people who felt the same as Revere did were known as Patriots. As tensions rose, so did the differences between Loyalists and Patriots.

Most people in Boston didn't want the troops there. There weren't enough barracks to hold them, so citizens were forced to

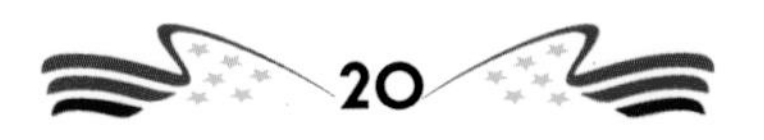

Paul Revere spent much of his life in this house on North Square. It is one of the most popular attractions on Boston's Freedom Trail, which connects many important Revolutionary sites.

allow the soldiers to stay in their homes. Also, because the troops received very little pay, some worked for Boston businesses when they weren't on duty. They were willing to work for very low wages. Many Boston citizens lost their jobs to the soldiers. Tensions between colonists and soldiers grew, until taunts and fistfights escalated to the Boston Massacre.

Soon after the Massacre, Revere and his family—which now included six children—moved to a new house in Old North Square. Built in 1680, the house still stands. It is the oldest house in downtown Boston and is a popular tourist attraction.

In May 1773, Sarah Revere died after giving birth. The baby lived only a few months. In October, Revere married Rachel Walker.

The marriage took place against a turbulent background. Parliament had recently passed the Tea Act. Once again, the citizens of Boston were outraged. Once again they took action.

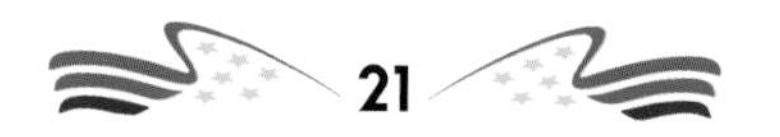

Ships carrying tea arrived in Boston at the end of November. No one would unload them. On the night of December 16, dozens of the Sons of Liberty, disguised as Native Americans, boarded the ships. They chopped open the crates of tea and dumped them into the harbor. The event became known as the Boston Tea Party. It is not known whether Revere participated. It is likely that he did.

Revere woke early the next morning. Boston's Patriot leaders wanted to make sure that the story had the proper spin in the rest of the colonies. They knew that people often believe the first version of a story, so they sent Revere to New York City on a fast horse.

Why Revere was selected for this vital mission is a bit of a mystery. Many men in Massachusetts grew up riding horses from a young age. Revere didn't. He didn't need a horse in his business: Most of his customers came to him, and Boston was small enough that he could walk if he had to make a delivery. It doesn't appear that he even owned a horse until sometime early in 1773, when there is a record of him building a barn for a mare he had just purchased. It must have been one of his very few luxuries. Between attending to his customers, serving as a husband and father, and meeting the demands of his revolutionary activities, Revere had little free time. He may have used some of it to ride his horse.

Historian Jayne Triber describes the qualities that must have set Revere apart from the region's other, perhaps slightly faster, horsemen: His "proven patriotism and valuable assistance to Boston's patriot leaders made him a trusted representative of Boston's Revolutionary movement. Revere could be relied upon to provide accurate information and informed political judgment both about events in Boston and the degree of support for his native town outside Massachusetts."[4]

When news of the "tea party" reached London, the British were outraged. Parliament imposed the Coercive Acts. While these new laws were directed against Boston, the government was sending a message to the other colonies as well: "Don't mess with us."

One of the acts ordered the citizens to repay the cost of the tea, which in today's currency would have been over half a million dollars. Boston Harbor would remain closed until they did. Bostonians refused to obey the order.

General Thomas Gage, commander in chief of the British Army in the colonies, was ordered to move his headquarters from New York City to Boston. He was also appointed as the new governor of Massachusetts.

Preparing for their defense, Patriots throughout Massachusetts formed militia companies. These companies began conducting regular military drills. Many set up depots to store ammunition and gunpowder.

Revere was frequently on the road. He carried messages to other cities, especially Philadelphia. He became the main source of news from Boston. The other colonies began to realize that what was happening in Boston could also happen to them.

In September 1774, British troops raided Charlestown and took the largest single store of gunpowder in Massachusetts. The militia, who believed the war had begun, started to march to Boston. They were called home. The incident became known as the Powder Alarm.

That month, representatives from the colonies met in Philadelphia for the First Continental Congress. The delegates agreed to support Boston if British troops made any attacks against the city. However, many of them insisted that the British would have to fire the first shots.

In Boston, Revere organized a group of about thirty men to keep an eye on what the British were doing. His spies often stayed up all night, walking through the shadows of the darkened town.

Their sleepless nights paid off. The British had a large store of ammunition in Fort William and Mary near Portsmouth, New Hampshire. There was only a handful of men guarding it. General Gage knew that the colonists were likely to make a move against the fort. He ordered his men to march to the fort and bring the ammunition back to Boston. Revere learned of Gage's plan. He sped to Portsmouth ahead of Gage's troops. The town's leaders sent several hundred armed men to the fort. The outnumbered British guards surrendered without firing any shots. The jubilant colonists removed the ammunition and hid it in other locations.

Even though hundreds of additional British soldiers had arrived in Boston, Gage didn't take any aggressive action. Months

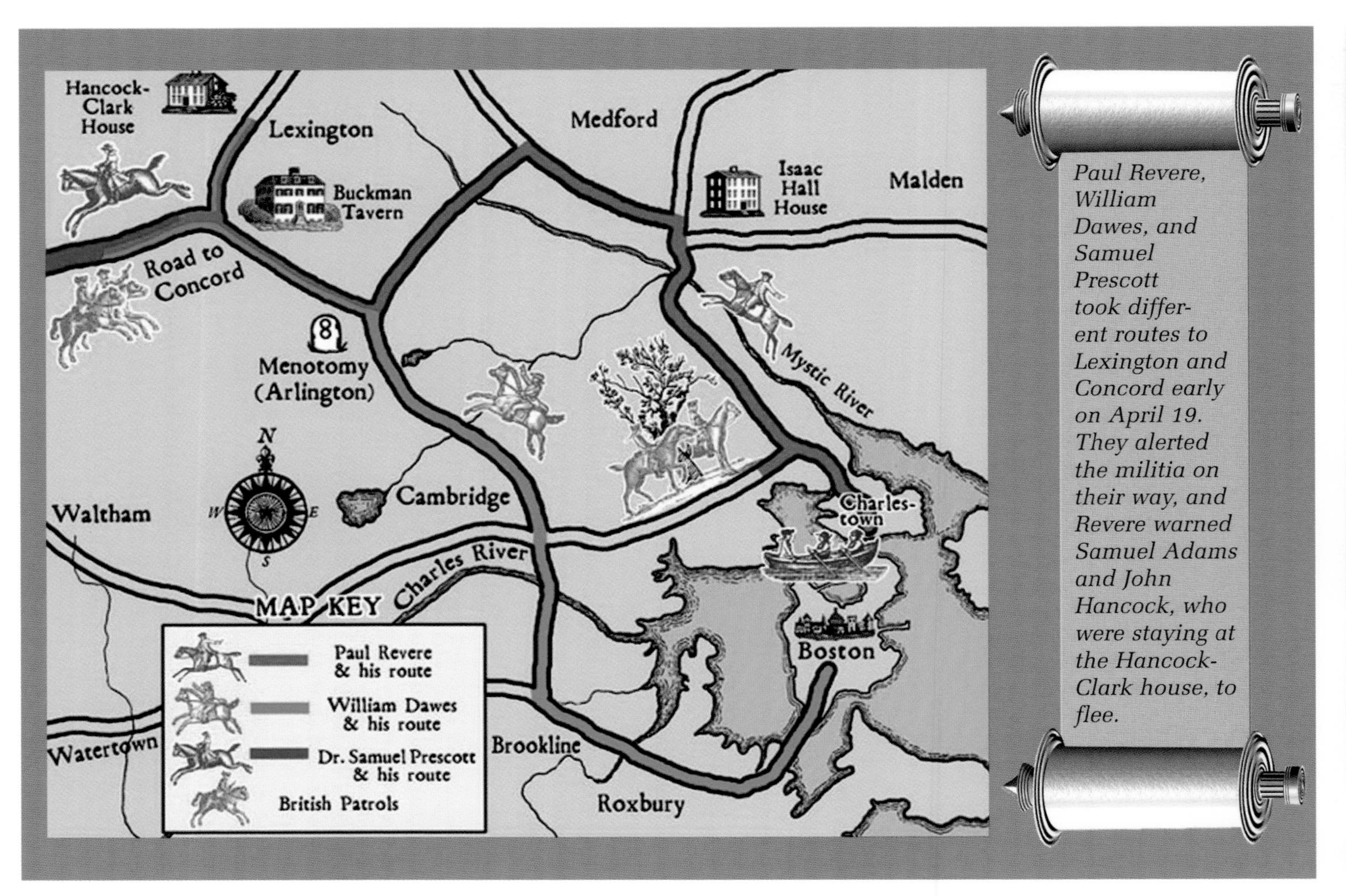

Paul Revere, William Dawes, and Samuel Prescott took different routes to Lexington and Concord early on April 19. They alerted the militia on their way, and Revere warned Samuel Adams and John Hancock, who were staying at the Hancock-Clark house, to flee.

went by. Samuel Adams was worried. If the uneasy peace held, the other colonies might withdraw their support. Boston would be on its own.

Despite his apparent calm, Gage was under pressure from the government in London to "get tough." He was urged to seize more of the Patriots' ammunition and to capture some of their leaders, especially John Hancock and Samuel Adams. These leaders would be placed on trial for treason. Most likely they would be found guilty and hanged. Gage began making secret plans—but word of his intentions leaked out in early April. Adams and Hancock fled from Boston to Lexington, a town about fifteen miles away.

Revere and Dr. Joseph Warren, another important leader, stayed behind to keep track of the British. They noticed that British scouts were on the roads between Boston and Concord, a town that contained a large store of ammunition. Revere rode to Concord to warn the town that British troops might soon be headed their way. Then he went to Lexington. He was certain that the British would stop there to try to capture Adams and Hancock.

On his way back to Boston, Revere stopped in Charlestown, across the Charles River from Boston. He knew security would be very tight when the troops made their move. He and Patriot leaders in Charlestown decided on a system of signals. "If the British went out by Water, we would [show] two [lanterns] in the North Church Steeple; and if by Land, one, as a Signal,"[5] he told them. That way a messenger could leave from Charlestown to warn of the approaching danger even if no one could get out of Boston.

The signals reflected the two British options for reaching Lexington. One was marching out of the city and around a broad, shallow bay. The other was to cross the bay in the boats taken from the warships anchored between Charlestown and Boston.

Loyalist spies told Gage that Concord had been alerted. The town's residents were beginning to move its ammunition. The general knew he had to move quickly. He also had to try to keep anyone from leaving Boston to raise further alarm. On the morning of April 18, he sent some of his best men to patrol the roads that linked Boston with Lexington and Concord. By then, the boats from two British warships had been launched and were tied up next to the vessels.

That evening, the crews of the British warships seized the colonists' ferries and other small boats that linked Boston and Charlestown. Anyone who tried to cross the river that night would be shot.

Warren was convinced that something was about to happen. He had an informant at the highest levels of the British troops. Although it would be dangerous to approach his source, he felt he had no choice. The informant confirmed his suspicion. The operation would begin within a few hours. The soldiers would proceed by boat across the bay. While no one is certain of the informant's identity, many historians believe that it was General Gage's wife, Margaret, who had been born and raised in New Jersey.

Hundreds of troops were assembling on Boston Common, with boats ready to take them across. Warren and Revere acted quickly. Warren sent William Dawes, another expert rider, to try to sneak through the British control point at Boston Neck. Dawes was successful. Once past the checkpoint, he spurred his horse toward Lexington.

Revere told three trusted friends that the soldiers were crossing the Charles River. They climbed into the steeple of Old North Church—about as high as a fifteen-story building—lit two lanterns, and shone them for a few seconds. Watchers in Charlestown saw the two faint lights. A waiting rider headed for Lexington. He never arrived. No one knows what happened to him.

Revere had hidden a rowboat on the Boston side of the Charles. The men from the warships hadn't found it. Two of his friends quietly rowed him across the river toward Charlestown. They had to pass close to the warships. It was a clear, moonlit night. They might be seen.

They weren't. Revere landed safely. Patriot leaders were waiting with a horse, Brown Beauty, who had a reputation for being especially fast.

What is probably the most famous ride in American history was about to get under way.

The Tea Act

Samuel Adams

In Paul Revere's era, tea was the most popular nonalcoholic beverage in the colonies. Despite their name, English coffeehouses primarily served tea. English settlers brought their fondness for the beverage with them across the Atlantic. Eventually the colonists were drinking even more tea than the British.

One reason the Townshend Acts of 1767 were so unpopular was that they included a tax on tea, making it more expensive. Though the other Townshend Acts were repealed, Parliament retained the tax on tea. In protest, the colonists refused to drink tea from England. Warehouses belonging to the East India Company, the primary British tea company, began filling up with unsold tea. The company was close to going out of business. Its directors appealed to Parliament for help.

The Tea Act of 1773 was the result. It allowed the East India Company to bring tea directly from India and China, making it cheaper. In addition, the tax was much lower than it had been under the terms of the Townshend Acts.

The Tea Act also gave the East India Company the right to select a few merchants to sell their tea. That angered many colonial businessmen, who could no longer sell tea. Some went out of business. It also angered American shipowners and sea captains. They were no longer able to transport tea.

The timing of the Tea Act was especially bad. In spite of the Boston Massacre, relations between the colonies and Britain had become relatively calm. Now the storm broke out again. The Tea Act led directly to the Boston Tea Party, which led to the harsh penalties imposed on Boston. The penalties in turn led to increasing outrage among the citizens and the rise in influence of revolutionary leaders such as John Hancock and Samuel Adams. Their increased importance made the British want to capture them. That set the events of Lexington and Concord in motion.

Paul Revere has awakened one of the minutemen whose house lay along his route. The minutemen were ready to spring into action. By daybreak thousands of them were awake and on their way to fight the British troops.

"The Shot Heard Round the World"

Early in the ride, Revere encountered two patrolling soldiers. One chased him, while the other raced ahead to cut him off. Revere escaped by galloping to another road that would also take him to Lexington.

He started awakening the colonists, setting in motion a detailed plan that Revere had helped to devise. One man couldn't arouse the entire countryside. Scores of men could. In each village and town along Revere's route, one man had been named a designated rider. That man's responsibility was to ride farther out into the countryside and awaken additional settlements. In turn, a man from each of those settlements would ride even farther and do the same thing.

The system was working. Thousands of men were soon awakened, some of them as far as thirty miles from Boston. They grimly picked up their rifles, kissed their families goodbye, and assembled on their village green. Then they marched toward Lexington and Concord. Not all of them would return.

In the meantime, the force of about 700 Redcoats had crossed the river and begun to march. Other than some of the officers, the men had no idea where they were going. Many had never been in battle before. They were about to get an education.

Revere rode into Lexington shortly after midnight. When he tried to alert Adams and Hancock, he was told that they had left orders not to allow any noise in the house.

"Noise," Revere replied. "You'll have noise enough before long. The regulars are coming out."[1] The sleeping men were quickly awakened.

A few minutes later, Dawes arrived. He and Revere decided to ride together to Concord. They were joined by Samuel Prescott, a Concord physician and a member of the Sons of Liberty. After a short ride, the men saw two soldiers on the road. Revere thought that he and his companions could overpower them. Suddenly four more soldiers, aiming pistols, emerged from the shadows. "If you go an inch further, you are a dead man,"[2] one of them told the three riders.

The soldiers ordered their captives to ride into a pasture. Prescott spurred his horse to leap over a fence and escaped. He continued on to Concord and aroused the town.

Revere spurred Brown Beauty toward a wood, but six more soldiers on horseback emerged. They captured him and ordered him off his horse. In the confusion, Dawes escaped. Moments later, he fell off his horse and limped back toward Lexington.

The soldiers were not in a kindly mood. "One of them . . . [clapped] his Pistol to my head, and said he was going to ask me some questions, if I did not tell the truth, he would blow my brains out,"[3] Revere wrote. He proudly informed the soldier who he was. He also boasted that the countryside was alarmed and awake. The British, who had captured four other men, decided to take their prisoners back to Lexington.

As they neared the town, they heard gunfire. Revere told them that the shots were intended to awaken even more people and summon them to Lexington and Concord. Then he tried to bluff the British. He told them that several hundred men would be waiting for them. The soldiers believed him. They let Revere and the other prisoners go. They thought it was more important to warn their army that the element of surprise had been lost.

Now free, Revere—who had been forced to give his horse to a soldier—continued on foot to Lexington to make sure that

Hancock and Adams had heeded his warning. They hadn't. The house was in an uproar. Hancock wanted to fight side by side with the militiamen. Adams kept trying to persuade him that he had far greater value as a Patriot leader. Revere told his story about being captured. That convinced Hancock. The three men hurried away in Hancock's ornate carriage. When he was sure that Hancock and Adams were safe, Revere returned to Lexington. He wanted to be where the action was.

There still was no sign of the British. Hancock's personal secretary, John Lowell, burst into the house where Revere was resting. In his hurry to leave, Hancock had left behind a trunk of important papers that contained the names of many Patriots. If the British found it, they would have enough evidence to convict those men of treason and hang them.

Revere and Lowell retrieved the heavy trunk. They were just in time. In the early morning light, Revere saw hundreds of Redcoats approaching. He and Lowell staggered down the stairs with their burden. They headed for a patch of woods where they could hide it. They were in plain sight of the Redcoats. Fortunately the troops were much more concerned with the Lexington militia facing them than with two men moving away from them.

Despite the alarm, only a few dozen militiamen had gathered on Lexington Common. Their leader, John Parker, realized his men were greatly outnumbered. They had no chance against the regulars, who were closing in on them. He ordered his men to stand aside and allow the regulars to pass. In the confusion, not everyone heard him. The first shot—or more likely shots—of the Revolutionary War rang out.

No one knows who fired first. Later, each side would accuse the other. Both sides would, however, agree on one thing: The initial gunfire didn't come from the British infantry troops or from Parker's men.

Historian Fischer notes, "What probably happened was this: several shots were fired close together—one from a mounted British officer, and another by an American spectator."[4] He further notes, "It is possible that one of these first shots was fired

At the beginning of the Battle of Lexington, a volley of musket fire from the British troops cut down more than a dozen Patriots. One British soldier was slightly wounded. The situation was very different a few hours later.

deliberately, either from an emotion of the moment, or from a cold-blooded intention to create an incident."[5]

The Patriot leaders knew that it had to seem as if the British had started the battle. That way they could claim self-defense—as they would when the battle was over. They therefore may have used a "plant." They knew that both sides would be under almost unbearable tension. In such a situation, the sound of an "accidental" gunshot would set things in motion.

The regulars were at a fever pitch. They had been marching for hours, carrying heavy packs. They began firing at the militiamen. Eight colonists died, and nine more were wounded. One man was bayoneted to death as he lay on the ground. Another was shot in

the chest while his wife watched in horror from their home. He crawled to his front door, where he died. One British soldier was slightly wounded.

The regulars ran after the fleeing militiamen, hoping to shoot them or kill them with bayonets, but the officers restored order. The British continued their march.

Revere and Lowell had been lucky. Hundreds of musket balls were flying through the air. They managed to reach the safety of the woods. Historians do not know what Revere did for the rest of that momentous day, but the forces he had set in motion would have profound consequences.

By the time the regulars reached Concord, the militia had retreated to the far side of the river that ran through the town. Several fires broke out in the town. Believing their homes were in danger, the militiamen hurried back toward the bridge they had just crossed. Apparently a few British soldiers panicked and fired their weapons. The militia fired back.

The incident became immortalized in 1837. Author Ralph Waldo Emerson wrote "Concord Hymn" when a memorial to the militiamen was dedicated in Concord. The most famous lines of the poem read: "Here once the embattled farmers stood:/And fired the shot heard round the world."[6]

Up to this point, the British had disrespected the colonial militia. Now they saw this so-called rabble moving toward them in disciplined formation, firing as they advanced.

Moments later, the unthinkable happened. British infantrymen were regarded as perhaps the world's finest soldiers. Some of them, under fire for the first time, ran away. Their officers finally gained control of the panicked men. By this time hundreds of militiamen were involved. They hid behind trees and large rocks on each side of the road and fired into the tightly packed regulars. More and more soldiers began to fall. British commander Colonel Francis Smith sent urgent messages back to Boston. With his losses mounting, he feared he could suffer a disastrous defeat.

The battle was becoming especially savage. The British were accustomed to fighting set-piece battles. In such conflicts, the opposing sides would march toward each other, shooting as they advanced. The British considered it cowardly that Patriots took shelter behind rocks and trees to shoot at them. They were angry because of what happened to one wounded regular. As he lay helpless, a militiaman attacked him with an ax. The soldier appeared to have been scalped.

The news spread through the ranks. Facts became distorted. One British officer later recorded that he was told "four men of the Fourth company [had been] killed and afterwards scalped, their eyes gouged, their noses and ears cut off.'"[7] That story wasn't true, but many regulars believed it. They adopted a fierce "take-no-prisoners" attitude during the rest of what became a long day.

As the regulars began the twenty-mile march toward the safety of Boston, they came under continuous fire. More and more were killed and wounded. As they approached Lexington, Parker and scores of grim men awaited them on a rocky hillside. They wanted payback. They badly wounded Colonel Smith, killed some of his men, and wounded still others. The hillside became known as Parker's Revenge.

Just past the hillside, the regulars saw what seemed a miraculous sight. Hundreds of fresh troops under the command of Lord Hugh Percy were waiting for them. Gage had ordered Percy to get under way at four that morning. Through a series of mistakes, Percy's column had been delayed for five hours. They had arrived just in time to save Smith's bedraggled soldiers from what could have been annihilation.

Percy reorganized the retreat and strengthened his defenses. Facing so many more enemy troops, it became harder for the militiamen to get close enough to attack. Finally, at about seven or eight in the evening, the tired and dispirited regulars arrived in Charlestown. They had been on their feet for almost a full day.

At that point, the militia broke off the attack. The exhausted Patriot riflemen looked at one another in awe. They had chased hundreds of British infantrymen back to Boston. What they probably didn't realize was that they had begun the struggle that would eventually create a new nation: the United States of America.

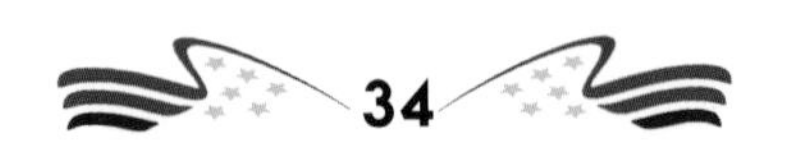

John Hancock

John Hancock

John Hancock was born in 1737 in Braintree (now Quincy), Massachusetts. His grandfather, father, and two uncles were all clergymen. Hancock took a different career path. His father died when he was still young. He was adopted by another uncle, Thomas Hancock, who had no children of his own. Thomas began his working life as an apprentice to a bookseller but became very wealthy as a shipowner and trader.

He encouraged John to attend Harvard College. After he graduated in 1754, John worked for his uncle, then went to England as Thomas's representative. Soon after he returned in 1764, his uncle died. As the only heir, John Hancock became the richest man in Massachusetts. Even though most of the people in his social circle were Loyalists, he soon became involved with Revolutionary politics.

Hancock used some of his wealth to finance the Patriots. After the Boston Massacre, he led a committee that demanded the removal of Governor Thomas Hutchinson. He also delivered a speech to commemorate the fourth anniversary of the event. The British general Gage regarded Hancock and Samuel Adams as the most dangerous men in Massachusetts.

In 1775, Hancock was elected president of the Second Continental Congress. It is likely that he would have preferred another position: commander-in-chief of the newly formed Continental Army. George Washington was selected instead.

Hancock was still president the following year when the Continental Congress adopted the Declaration of Independence. He was the first signer, and his signature is the largest on the document. Because his signature was so bold, even today many people say, "Put your John Hancock here" when they ask someone to sign a document.

Hancock left the Congress in 1777 because of ill health. He was elected as the first governor of the state of Massachusetts in 1780. He was reelected four more times, then retired. He returned to political life in the same post in 1787. He used his influence to persuade Massachusetts to ratify the proposed U.S. Constitution. He remained governor until his death in 1793.

Paul Revere's portrait painted by Charles Saint-Memin around 1800. By this time Revere had become a successful businessman.

CHAPTER 5

Remembering Revere

To win the battle of public opinion, Patriot leaders quickly collected firsthand stories about Lexington and Concord. The British had fired first, they maintained. They were only defending their property and their lives. One newspaper referred to the "Bloody Butchery by the British Troops" and, across the top of the page, printed two rows of coffins symbolizing dead Patriots. The leaders sent these accounts to England, hoping they would arrive before General Gage's official report.

It was just as important to tell the rest of the colonies what had happened. Once again, Revere played a major role as a courier, riding to many different places for more than a week. Historian William H. Hallahan notes, "He acquired an odor so gamy [rotten] that his associates tried to conduct all meetings with him out of doors."[1]

A month later, Rachel and the children were able to leave Boston. The reunited family settled in Watertown, several miles outside the city.

Revere soon had other important work to do. The rebels needed paper money. Revere's skill with engraving made him a natural choice to print it.

Revere tried to join the Continental Army as an officer. He was rejected. Washington and the other leaders wanted men with military experience who were also gentlemen—meaning that they had a high social position, money, and education. Revere didn't qualify. Another reason was political. Not everyone trusted men from Boston or even from most of New England.

Two months after Lexington, the two sides fought the Battle of Bunker Hill. Though the British lost hundreds of soldiers, the militiamen ran out of ammunition. The British captured the hill. Joseph Warren was killed. The doctor had been Revere's closest

The Battle of Bunker Hill was decided when the colonists ran out of ammunition. British troops poured into the colonial positions with fixed bayonets. They were angry with the severe losses they had suffered. They took few prisoners.

friend among the Revolutionary leaders. Two years later, Revere would name a son after his fallen friend.

On March 17, 1776, the British evacuated Boston. Revere and his family were able to return. His fellow citizens named him to a number of important positions in the city. He also became a lieutenant colonel in the Massachusetts Artillery Regiment. In 1779, he was part of what became known as the Penobscot Expedition. It was a mission to capture a British fort in Maine. It failed. Revere was fired from the militia. He made several efforts to clear his name, and was finally successful in 1782.

At that point, the two warring sides were trying to agree on peace terms. The British had surrendered at the battle of Yorktown in October 1781. After lengthy negotiations, a treaty was signed in 1783.

Boston began to prosper again. Revere's silversmith shop had not done well during the war. After the war, new clients replaced the ones he had lost. The shop expanded. Revere gave most of the work to his apprentices. His oldest son, Paul Revere Jr., became responsible for the shop's daily operations.

Then Revere tried other businesses. The first was a hardware store. He had problems importing many of the goods he wanted to sell and eventually closed it.

His other ventures were more successful. Taking advantage of the booming shipbuilding industry, he opened a foundry near the harbor. He forged raw materials such as iron into bolts, nails, and other pieces of hardware necessary to build ships.

Four years later, he began casting church bells. Hundreds of his bells were hoisted into New England steeples to summon worshipers. He also cast cannons.

In 1800, Revere converted a mill into a factory and became the first American to roll out thin sheets of copper. The most important use of these sheets was to cover the hulls of ships. The sheeting made the ships faster. Some of his copper sheets lined the bottom of the USS *Constitution.* The frigate eventually became the most famous ship in the history of the U.S. Navy. He also used his copper sheeting to cover the dome of the Massachusetts State House.

Paul Revere ventured into businesses that would help the shipbuilding industry. First, his foundry made fasteners and other hardware. Then he opened a factory that made copper sheeting, which was used to cover ships' hulls.

Revere finally retired in 1811 and turned his businesses over to his son Joseph Warren Revere. Two years later, his wife and his eldest son died. On May 10, 1818, Paul Revere died of natural causes. One local newspaper commented, "His country found him one of her most zealous and active of her sons."[2] He was never forgotten in the Boston area, but hardly anyone in the rest of the country had heard of him.

Several decades later, when the country was about to be ripped apart by the Civil War, poet Henry Wadsworth Longfellow resurrected Revere's memory. Longfellow wanted to remind his readers about how the colonies had joined together in order to win their independence. He decided to focus on Revere's ride as a symbol of the heroism behind that struggle. It was a somewhat ironic choice. Longfellow's grandfather had been a general involved

in dismissing Revere from the Massachusetts militia after the Penobscot Expedition.

Longfellow was already famous throughout the United States for his long poems *Evangeline*, *Hiawatha,* and the *Courtship of Miles Standish*. His new poem, "The Midnight Ride of Paul Revere," was an instant sensation. The name of Paul Revere became known all over the United States. For many years, children were taught to memorize at least the first stanza of the poem:

> Listen, my children, and you shall hear
> Of the midnight ride of Paul Revere,
> On the eighteenth of April, in Seventy-five;
> Hardly a man is now alive
> Who remembers that famous day and year.[3]

There are some factual errors in the poem. Revere's capture is not mentioned. Neither are Dawes and Prescott. Longfellow probably wasn't very concerned with accuracy. Under the threat of Civil War, the country's unity was slipping away. Longfellow wanted the country to stay together, and to point out that individuals could still make a difference. The poem concludes:

> Through all our history, to the last,
> In the hour of darkness and peril and need,
> The people will waken and listen to hear
> The hurrying hoof-beats of that steed,
> And the midnight message of Paul Revere.[4]

Longfellow failed in one sense. In April 1861, guns began booming at Fort Sumter in South Carolina, starting the Civil War. Hundreds of thousands of soldiers and civilians died over the next four years.

But Longfellow fully succeeded in another sense. He created an image of the lone individual risking his life to do what needs to be done. This image has become one of the most enduring in American history. As a result, millions of Americans continue to remember the courageous Paul Revere.

The USS *Constitution*

USS Constitution

During the last years of the eighteenth century, American merchant ships in the Mediterranean Sea were frequently captured by pirates from the coast of North Africa. In 1794, Congress decided to build six frigates to reduce the threat. Designer Joshua Humphrey made these frigates strong enough to fight on even terms with much larger warships, yet fast enough to keep up with smaller vessels. He used live oak, a tree native only to American forests, for the planking. In some places, the planking was seven inches thick.

The USS *Constitution*, one of the six frigates, was launched in 1797. The hull was protected by Revere's copper sheeting. She sailed in the Mediterranean, helping to reduce the pirate problems. She became immortal in the War of 1812. Except for the victory of John Paul Jones against Britian's *Serapis,* the record of American ships during the Revolutionary War was dismal. In 1812, British captains had no reason to expect anything different this time. They were in for a rude shock.

Soon after the start of the war, *Constitution* met the British frigate *Guerriere* in the open sea. *Guerriere* supposedly had equal firepower. She didn't. In a twenty-minute battle, *Constitution* crippled her opponent by knocking down all three masts. *Guerriere*'s return fire caused little damage. One cannon ball bounced off *Constitution*'s thick planking. An American sailor called out, "Huzzah! Her sides are made of iron!" Ever since then, the ship has been nicknamed "Old Ironsides."

Her victory was a stunning achievement for the U.S. Navy. Four months later, *Constitution* defeated another British frigate, the *Java*. Shortly before the end of the war, she took on two British ships at the same time and defeated both of them.

After the war, the *Constitution* lay idle. In 1830, the Navy decided to scrap her. The plan horrified Oliver Wendell Holmes, a young law student. He wrote a poem called "Old Ironsides," praising the ship. The poem raised a national outcry and the vessel was preserved. Today the ship remains afloat in Boston Harbor. Tens of thousands of visitors tour her every year.

Chapter Notes

Chapter 1: A Quarrel Snowballs

1. David Hackett Fischer, *Paul Revere's Ride* (New York: Oxford University Press, 1994), p. 23.

Chapter 2: The Man of the House

1. Esther Forbes, *Paul Revere and the World He Lived In* (Boston: Houghton Mifflin Company, 1942), pp. 31–32.
2. Ibid., p. 32.
3. Ibid., p. 131–132.

Chapter 3: The Gathering Storm

1. Jayne E. Triber, *A True Republican: The Life of Paul Revere* (Amherst, Massachusetts: The University of Massachusetts Press, 1998), p. 64.
2. David Hackett Fischer, *Paul Revere's Ride* (New York: Oxford University Press, 1994), p. 22.
3. Ibid.
4. Triber, p. 198.
5. Ibid., p. 102

Chapter 4: "The Shot Heard Round the World"

1. Jayne E. Triber, *A True Republican: The Life of Paul Revere* (Amherst, Massachusetts: The University of Massachusetts Press, 1998), p. 103.
2. Paul Revere, "Memorandum on Events of April 18, 1775," from John Rhodehamel, editor, *The American Revolution: Writings from the War of Independence* (New York: The Library of America, 2001), p. 2.
3. Ibid.
4. David Hackett Fischer, *Paul Revere's Ride* (New York: Oxford University Press, 1994), p. 194.
5. Ibid.
6. Ralph Waldo Emerson, "The Concord Hymn," http://www.nps.gov/mima/hymn.htm
7. David Hackett Fischer, *Paul Revere's Ride* (New York: Oxford University Press, 1994), p. 218.

Chapter 5: Remembering Revere

1. William H. Hallahan, *The Day the American Revolution Began: 19 April 1775* (New York: William Morrow, 2000), p. 92.
2. Jayne E. Triber, *A True Republican: The Life of Paul Revere* (Amherst, Massachusetts: The University of Massachusetts Press, 1998), p. 195.
3. Henry Wadsworth Longfellow, *The Midnight Ride of Paul Revere* (Brooklyn, New York: Handprint Books, 2001), p. 6.
4. Ibid., p. 28.

Chronology

1734	Paul Revere born in late December in Boston, Massachusetts
1750	Along with five other boys, signs the Bell Ringers Agreement
1754	Takes over family business when his father dies
1756	Takes part in military expedition during French and Indian War
1757	Marries Sarah Orne
1758	Daughter Deborah is born
1760	Son Paul Jr. is born
1765	Helps form the Sons of Liberty in Boston
1768	Makes engraving of British soldiers landing in Boston
1770	Makes engraving of Boston Massacre
1773	Wife, Sarah, dies; marries Rachel Walker; probably participates in Boston Tea Party
1775	Makes ride in early morning hours of April 19 to warn colonists about approaching British troops
1776	Appointed lieutenant colonel in Massachusetts militia
1777	Son Joseph Warren is born
1779	Dismissed from militia after failure of Penobscot Expedition
1782	Formal hearing clears his name of wrongdoing in connection with Penobscot Expedition
1788	Opens foundry in converted mill
1792	Begins casting church bells
1800	Opens copper rolling mill
1811	Retires from his various businesses
1813	Wife, Rachel, and son Paul Jr. die
1818	Dies on May 10 in Boston

Timeline in History

1630 Boston is founded.
1682 William Penn lays out the city of Philadelphia.
1685 Persecution of Huguenots in France resumes after nearly a century of relative peace.
1719 English author Daniel Defoe writes *Robinson Crusoe.*
1731 Benjamin Franklin founds the first American public library.
1735 John Adams, who will sign the Declaration of Independence and become the second U.S. President, is born.
1756 The French and Indian War is officially declared; it ends seven years later.
1760 George III becomes the British King.
1765 British Parliament passes the Stamp Act.
1775 George Washington becomes commander in chief of the Continental Army.
1778 The French sign Treaty of Alliance with the United States.
1781 British General Cornwallis surrenders to a combined American and French army in the last major battle of the Revolutionary War.
1783 The Treaty of Paris ends the Revolutionary War and marks the independence of the former colonies from Britain.
1789 The U.S. Constitution is adopted and becomes the law of the land; George Washington becomes the first U.S. President.
1792 The first two political parties in the United States are formed: Republican (led by Thomas Jefferson) and Federalist (led by John Adams).
1812 The War of 1812 against the British begins.
1818 British author Mary Wollstonecraft Shelley writes *Frankenstein.*
1830 Oliver Wendell Holmes writes the poem "Old Ironsides," which saves the USS *Constitution* from being scrapped.
1848 The discovery of gold in California leads to a rush of prospectors the following year.
1860 Henry Wadsworth Longfellow writes "The Midnight Ride of Paul Revere"; it is published in 1861.
1865 The Civil War ends.
1876 George Armstrong Custer and five companies under his command are annihilated by Native Americans in the Battle of Little Bighorn.
1882 Henry Wadsworth Longfellow dies.

Further Reading

For Young Adults

Grote, JoAnn. *Paul Revere: American Patriot.* Philadelphia: Chelsea House Publishers, 2000.

King, David. *Lexington and Concord.* Brookfield, Connecticut: Twenty-First Century Books, 1997.

Phelan, Mary Kay. *Midnight Alarm: The Story of Paul Revere's Ride.* New York: Thomas Y. Crowell, 1968.

Randolph, Ryan. *Paul Revere and the Minutemen of the American Revolution.* New York: Rosen Publishing Group, 2002.

Sutcliffe, Jane. *Paul Revere.* Minneapolis, Minnesota: Lerner Publishing Company, 2002.

Wadsworth, Henry Longfellow. *The Midnight Ride of Paul Revere.* Brooklyn, New York: Handprint Books, 2001.

Whitelaw, Nancy. *The Shot Heard Round the World: The Battles of Lexington and Concord.* Greensboro, North Carolina: Morgan Reynolds, 2001.

Works Consulted

Beach, Edward L. *The United States Navy.* New York: Henry Holt and Company, 1986.

Fischer, David Hackett. *Paul Revere's Ride.* New York: Oxford University Press, 1994.

Forbes, Esther. *Paul Revere and the World He Lived In.* Boston: Houghton Mifflin Company, 1942.

Hallahan, William H. *The Day the American Revolution Began: 19 April 1775.* New York: William Morrow, 2000.

Rhodehamel, John (editor). *The American Revolution: Writings from the War of Independence.* New York: The Library of America, 2001.

Triber, Jayne E. *A True Republican: The Life of Paul Revere.* Amherst: The University of Massachusetts Press, 1998.

On the Internet

The Paul Revere House http://www.paulreverehouse.org

Paul Revere—Midnight Rider http://www.cvesd.k12.ca.us/finney/paulvm/paulvm.html

Gioia, Dana. "On 'Paul Revere's Ride' by Henry Wadsworth Longfellow. http://www.danagioia.net/essays/elongfellow.htm

Banner, David. "Boston History." http://www.searchboston.com/history.html

Boston History http://www.bostontravelguide.com/boston_history.html

The History of Tea http://www.stashtea.com/facts.htm

"The American Revolution: Tea Act, May 10, 1773." http://www.u-s-history.com/pages/h1248.html

Linder, Doug. "The Boston Massacre Trials: An Account." http://www.law.umkc.edu/faculty/projects/ftrials/bostonmassacre/bostonaccount.html

"The Boston Massacre: A Behind-the-Scenes Look at Paul Revere's Most Famous Engraving." http://earlyamerica.com/review/winter96/massacre.html

Emerson, Ralph Waldo. "The Concord Hymn." http://www.nps.gov/mima/hymn.htm

Glossary

apprentice (uh-PREN-tus)
a person legally bound to another person for a specified period of time to learn a trade or craft.

barracks (BAA-ruks)
buildings used to house soldiers.

constituents (kun-STIT-choo-unts)
people who live in the same electoral district.

engraving (in-GRAY-ving)
a etching of a design onto a material such as copper; the design can be reproduced by stamping it onto paper.

foundry (FOWN-dree)
a place where metal is melted and formed into various shapes.

frigate (FRIH-gut)
a medium-sized sailing warship especially noted for its speed.

Huguenots (HYOO-guh-nots)
the leading Protestant group in France who, during the 1700s, were executed or forced to leave the country.

Loyalist (LOY-uh-list)
a colonist who remained loyal to the king.

manslaughter (MAN-slaw-ter)
a crime in which a person is killed, usually accidentally, the penalties are less than those for murder.

Patriot (PAY-tree-ut)
a colonist who wanted America to be independent of Britain.

regulars (REH-gyoo-lurs)
soldiers in the British Army.

spin
the presenting of a set of facts to fit a certain point of view.

undaunted (un-DON-tud)
not discouraged in spite of encountering difficulties.

Index